Out of Nashoba

Out of Nashoba

Poems by

Jonathan Clark Patrick

© 2024 Jonathan Clark Patrick. All rights reserved.
This material may not be reproduced in any form, published,
reprinted, recorded, performed, broadcast,
rewritten, or redistributed without
the explicit permission of Jonathan Clark Patrick.
All such actions are strictly prohibited by law.

Cover design by Shay Culligan
Cover image by Robert Anthony Henry
Author photo by Celia McLaughlin Patrick

ISBN: 978-1-63980-605-8
Library of Congress Control Number: 2023525696

Kelsay Books
502 South 1040 East, A-119
American Fork, Utah 84003
Kelsaybooks.com

In memory of
Robert Anthony Henry
December 7, 1949–April 4, 1998

Acknowledgments

The quotes in the poem "The Jebel es Zubleh" are from *Ben-Hur: A Tale of the Christ,* Dover Thrift Editions, 2015, an unabridged republication of the work originally published in 1880 by Harper & Brothers, New York

"He Took Off the Old Coat" was inspired by "Two Coats" from the album *Mountain Soul* by Patty Loveless.

"No Tear Goes Wasted," "Nashoba Waters," "Dance Lessons," and "Trespassing in Reed's Grain Mill" first appeared in *The Prairie Review,* Spring 2024.

Cover image is by Robert Anthony Henry (circa 1975) and is from an undated card to the author celebrating New Year's Day.

Contents

Out of Nashoba

Out of Nashoba	15
Leeway	16
Six Stitches	17
Airplanes	18
The Tire Swing	20
Trespassing in Reed's Grain Mill	21
The Shed in Jenks' Orchard	23
The Clubhouse on Nash Road	25

Nashoba Ruins

The Lean-To	29
Ritz Crackers	30
Bicycle Racing, Mount Hope Cemetery	31
The Jebel es Zubleh	32
Sledding	33
Hockey on Meadow Ice	34
Stripping Paint	35
Life Insurance	36
The Fish Store	38
Dance Lessons	39
Engineer's Boots	41
Quarry Lands	42
Twenty-One Windows	44
1969	46
A Boy's Dream of Quicksand	47
Nashoba Ruins	48

Rob

Rob	51
Letters from Rob	53

He Took Off the Old Coat

The Carriage House	63
Stone Wall, Poetry	64
Haggling	65
The Fence on Sedgewick Drive	66
Abandonment	67
Waiting for Owls	68
Nashoba Waters	69
No Tear Goes Wasted	70
Crows Crowded into the Redwood Tree Tops	71
He Took Off the Old Coat	72

Out of Nashoba

Out of Nashoba

Amber-set in Nashoba time, parents,
Eddie and Dot, divining the Boy's way,
ensuring his college years, and a job
better than watch-repairer or milkman.

The Boy working his teenage persona,
when lives lived were not memes or metaphors
co-opted by the political class
and professional "working-class" liars.

Muscle cars, American Flyer sleds,
hockey on iced marshes, "Surfin' USA,"
"She Loves You," "Satisfaction" on AM,
sunset trips, Kimballs' ice cream in sugar cones.

All chapters in a Coming-of-Age story,
the Boy tiptoeing in the etched traces
of New England giants, literati,
headstones carved by the swords of archangels.

Leeway

Many leagues from his origins
and the certainty of Nashoba,
his memories adrift on measured currents
crossed, wind speed, atmospheric flows,
depressions of the heart in search
of lasting friendships, years waning,
the frothy crests of successes
in his mature years, commitments.
In hindsight's navigation,
his coursing revealed,
surrendering to maelstroms
and becalming aftermaths,
anchoring, Boy to Man, Poet.

Six Stitches

Six stitches in the Boy's chin, a tale told
of upending his Ford pedal tractor,
wobbly when cornering on braided rugs,
while racing with Brother Ed, on his Schwinn
roadster, claiming ignorance of his foul—
despite the two-inch scar and cross-hatching.
The collision, the Boy, unseated, head
over heels, onto the hearth fence Eddie
fashioned from a forged steel wagon wheel rim.
Neither Dot nor Eddie, long passed on,
alive to bear witness to the fidelity
of the Man's oral histories—his song
of youth, or a fabulist's yarn cloaking
a fall learning to ride a trike?
The first, the Man wondered,
of many conceits that masked falling short,
not quite telling the whole story?

Airplanes

Boomer men love their boyhood toys,
collect them now, timeline artifacts
burnished in memory's guardianship.
The Man, not immune to nostalgia
remembered his boyhood airplanes
hung from dropped ceiling tiles
with monofilament line—modeling flight.

The Super Constellation, Line Mar, props
bellyaching, running lights blinking red
as it flew across the floor, under the bed,
in shadows, the Boy entranced,
the friction engine unwinding, lights
gently failing, scrambling over to recover
and rewind, three strokes to get up to speed,
then back along the same flight path;

The F-106 Delta Dart model,
a birthday gift, visiting Grandma Grace,
from Woolworth's on Moody Street;
Easily 50 pieces, Monogram,
with USAF decals, red, white, and blue.
The Boy, clumsy with glue and paint,
took his time, followed the instructions
accounting for every piece, organized
on the kitchen table, Step One, Step Two;

The Cleveland Models P-38 Lightning
assembled from die-cut Balsa parts,
painstakingly gluing elevators,
struts, ailerons, wing ribs, and dual rudders,
the fuselage frame enveloped in lacquered
tissue paper, painted in WWII camouflage;

The Mercury-Redstone rocket, Revell,
red escape tower, Freedom 7 capsule
and the *Into Space* booklet included.
The Boy imagining he was Shepard
at the controls for those fifteen minutes
and twenty-two seconds, 5,000 mph,
100 miles above his Nashoba home.

The Old Man thought about his exodus
from Nashoba and middle-class limits,
his boyish aspirations invested
in toy airplanes and model space rockets,
compared to the ease of his retirement,
the years invested in ensuring comfort,
the thousands of fifteen-minute flights
he took to achieve escape velocity
from the gravity of home and boyhood.

The Tire Swing

The Boy, second grade, all of sixty pounds,
straying where the teenagers hung a swing,
a tractor tire tethered to a two-inch
hawser in the corner of the remains
of an apple orchard, the farmland sold,
"improved," now the Boy's neighborhood, his home,
the farmhouse, the barn, some aged apple trees,
bordering oaks, sheltering the ruins.
Shinnying up to a broad branch ten feet
above the decades of compacted earth
abused by farm machinery, and boys,
the swing just out of his reach, the taunting,
bullies teasing the Boy to jump, to grab the rope,
to swing, and, in a boasting interval,
confident he could make the jump, he jumped,
mistimed the swinging tire, falling, crashing
to the root-hard ground, fracturing his wrist,
took home his badge—a pink cast for three months.

Trespassing in Reed's Grain Mill

Ten years old, we itched for adventure,
squirming inside Reed's Grain Mill, cavernous,
through a breach where the paint-worn doors,
hung from iron trolleys cast before the Wars,
bowed, weather-warped, from their frames;
Grinding equipment and machine shop long sold off,
now garaging Old Man Laffin's hoard, vintage
vehicles retired before the Boy's Nashoba childhood,
those still running, flaunted in town parades,
others in parts, suspended animation
garaged in the gloaming, longing for drivers
dead for decades, running board to running board,
chrome grill to rumble seat and spare tire, stored.

Pulleyed lifts, industrial age wizardry,
towered above us hitched to oak joists,
hand-hewn, heartwood white when sawn,
a century of summer roasts and winter freezes,
dowels hammered true, through tenons adzed,
raised and lowered the cars.

We trespassed through the stalls,
our underage ambitions, secretive,
pretending to drive one of the monsters,
sitting on the cloth seats, threadbare, hands gripping
the golden mahogany steering wheels.

The chestnut floors supporting
Packard Twelves and Four Hundreds,
Studebaker Hawks, Hudsons and Nashes,
Ford Big Jobs, Deuces, Model As and Ts,
Pontiac Streamliners, Chieftans, Torpedos
Chevrolet Bel Airs, Nomads,

Cadillac La Salles, Eldorados,
Buick Roadmasters, Specials and Limiteds,
Oldsmobile Vikings and Series 60s,
Dodge Royals, DeSoto Pacesetters,
Chrysler Imperials and Airflows
steel pressed and cast, cars with curves
and chrome, dashboards walnut, worked by hand.

The Shed in Jenks' Orchard

At the northeast corner
of Jenks' collapsing orchard—
the apple trees storm-split, ruined,
tractor ruts walkable, pathing,
beneath branches we skulked,
the track reddened helter-skelter
by fruit persisting, falling fulfilled
from withered branches.

There was an abandoned shed,
constructed for Nashoba winters,
with a roof of tarpaper and tin,
a rusting combination lock
securing the corrugated door,
and a double hung window, aged,
the boy wedged open, ghostly,
with a bar from the farm's scrapheap,
scavenging his fathers' dreams.

Dozens of radios—
Majestic, Crosley,
RCA, Emerson,
Philco, Westinghouse,
Silvertone and Truetone—
stored on shelves pieced together
from construction leftovers.

Amidst tubes, condensers, spare knobs,
wire harnesses, rolls of friction tape,
shrouded in decades of dust, spider-silk,
starling and field mouse droppings.

The Boy, in mid-morning meditations,
conjured the blush of the Zenith's dial
in his bedroom, the hum and hiss, the glow—
in the dark, safe, alone but connected—
and a hockey announcer's play-by-play,
amplified, waves of crackling electrons transduced,
Boom Boom to Beliveau to The Rocket . . .
Score!

The Clubhouse on Nash Road

The Boy and his brother helped Eddie build
a clubhouse hugging the Nash Road fencing,
8x12 joists laid across concrete blocks
keeping the hoarfrost and groundwater out.

They played whist in the sputtering blush
of oil lamps, sleeping on cots beneath nets,
mosquitos owning Nashoba summers.

Eddie organized his tools on pegboards
where in white paint he outlined hacksaws, squares,
framing hammers, ordered, small to large.

His Craftsman lathe, table saw and band saw,
powered miter box for compound angles
stood cleaned and oiled after every project.

The clapboard siding, asphalt-shingled roof,
two double-hung windows, well-framed door,
brass hinges and a Yale dead bolt and lock.

We learned shingling, using flooring jacks
to tighten oak planks, setting finish nails
in fascia boards to prepare the pine for painting—
club house long gone, hard work, its own reward.

Nashoba Ruins

The Lean-To

Just after sunrise, late August, the boys
from the neighborhood shadowed Fort Pond Brook,
keeping northwest of the wetlands, hunting
for unexplored ground for their lean-to fort;
Decided on a span of pines, twelve foot
wide, sufficient to warrant the crossbeam
bearing the construct of white pine branches
and fishbone ferns, Scotch pine needles, bog moss
prized from the freshwater marsh bare-handed,
molasses-slow, the thick current draining
to the Assabet River, accepting
cattails and rushes, river offerings.
Home base secured, the boys architectured
a throwing-stick course, using felled pine roots
shaped like war clubs, polished, painted fiercely—
retrievable after an errant throw.
In that dim world, fit for owls, for hours,
acres of dry rot, pine decay, pine straw
littered with branches, barked and bleached, rarely
a shaft of light bold enough to inspire
a blush of Lady Slipper or Witch's Glove,
there was self-determination in stick games—
absent striped fields or fences, umpires, coaches,
freed of parents obsessing over calls,
working the refs, heckling the other team,
just a made-up game in the woods with friends.

Ritz Crackers

Sunday morning after Mass
Eddie ferried us to Concord,
his '61 Plymouth Suburban, black,
taillights like Sidewinder missiles
slung under swept-back wings,
to Mr. Gordon's, a travel agent,
house-sitting his avocation,
ambition traded for security,
unconcerned with saving the world.

Mr. Gordon served us Ritz Crackers,
cucumber slices and duck pâté;
He and Eddie fretting over
The New York Times crossword.

The Boy exploring the master bedrooms
on a quest to decipher Concordia's secrets,
reluctant to reveal his finds,
but caressing the walnut panels,
the embroidered coverlets, silk;
Lurking in the bathroom where the cedar
and lavender scent of hand-crafted soaps lingered;
Opening breakfront doors,
prowling a world foreign to Nashoba,
his home, innocent of capitalist lust.

Bicycle Racing, Mount Hope Cemetery

The second-hand Schwinn Cruiser, his first bike,
balloon tires, white-walled, no posh derailleurs
or handbrakes like the sleek Peugot ten-speeds
the Acton Center kids rode, built to last
with panniers perfect for the paper route
the Boy worked a few weeks each year, on call
when the girl, a townie from West Acton,
long-limbed and slim, hard but not a player,
living with her mother, needed a hand.

The Boy was cautious when working near her—
she, a head or more taller, older he thought
but he never had the courage to ask her age
since she always seemed on-the-boil
a breath away from an outburst, a punch
or shove—head down, in silence, folded
The Boston Globes and *Herald Americans*
securing them with elastic bands, filled
his two baskets and followed the route
she had carefully written out for him.

Racing our bikes on the headstone pathways
in Mount Hope, centuries old, rough-hewn
low stone walls and modest cast-iron gate,
welcoming both visitor and vagrant,
the single room clapboard chapel, white-washed,
with its Craftsman fieldstone chimney and porch,
close guarded by a wildflower garden.
Grounds expanding into the white pine woods.
three thousand souls beneath red oak and ash,
the beech canopy over the first stones
sixty feet high, planted two centuries
before meadow became small town graveyard
on the road linking West and South Acton.

The Jebel es Zubleh

Fifth grade, first semester, the C+ in penmanship,
Eddie and Dot ballistic, in a punishing mood,
the Boy would copy, long hand, in blue books,
Ben-Hur, a paperback, abridged version
Eddie bought admiring Heston's Judah.

The Jebel es Zubleh is a mountain
fifty miles and more in length, and so narrow
that its tracery on the map
gives it a likeness to a caterpillar
crawling from the south to the north.

Daily the Boy dutifully transcribed
The Tale of the Christ, reveling in the poetry
of Roman charioteers and wrecked triremes,
Jerusalem and matched Arabian stallions,
amid the fiction of political betrayal, faith.

It may be supposed the dullest of them poising his oar,
thought of all that might happen, yet could promise himself
nothing; for victory would but rivet his chains the firmer,
while the chances of the ship were his;
sinking or on fire, he was doomed to her fate.

Some dozens of pages done, Eddie and Dot agreed
the Boy had served his sentence, the book returned
to Eddie's office, reshelved beside Gibbon's *Fall,*
and the Boy, on probation, finished reading the tale,
discovering Ben-Hur's triumph in the Circus.

Decades later, his free writing legible
when he focused, the Man preserved
his own thoughts, drafts, and chronicles
in cursive in a series of college-ruled notebooks,
worrying fragments into verse.

Sledding

The Boy in Nashoba late winter,
his Honor Class memo arriving
like a message from Starfleet Academy,
embarrassed, tried to tell his neighbor
as they saucered together the hill;
She, feigning indifference,
her father taking the family South
where General Motors was still hiring.

The Boy cursed, clever but undisciplined,
forever different, other, not,
he caromed downhill,
the saucer with a mind of its own.

The Others, on their Flexible Flyers,
runners waxed like skis,
the Arrow & Eagle scraped and worn
from the brass buttons and buckles
of winter coats and boots,
navigating the snow trail
through the close pines,
bursting into a meadow
flooded, frozen and predestined.

The Boy, sled-less, never finding his way
to glassy surfaces, frictionless,
forever sliding, the horizon expanding,
the young willows by the river's edge,
ice sheathed, bent, accepting the sun.

He shouldered his saucer,
Retraced the path cresting Thurston's Hill
And pitched himself down slope.

Hockey on Meadow Ice

Winter for us was hockey
on meadow ice scoured of night-snow,
hardening beneath the Nashoba sky.

Neighborhood teams, pickup games,
no lifting or slap shots,
in a roughly rectangular rink,
marsh grass hummocks
and cranberry tangle boards,
playing round-robin weekend tournaments
without linesmen, just skating,
sandwiches in cartooned lunch boxes
or brown paper bags.

The slow march home
through woods at dusk,
leaning into January gusts,
iced jeans stiff at boot-tops—
retelling stories of shots and saves,
trash-talking bad passes,
craving Bobby Hull's curved blade,
whiffing on the one-timer,
a blizzard of excuses implicating
bad sticks, bad ice, Tacks vs. Bauers—
skates tied onto old-school Sher-Wood sticks,
left or right, shouldered, as if a platoon,
returning, bone-sore after patrolling.

Stripping Paint

The memory of stripping paint,
boys on a homemade scaffold—
2x4's fastened into 4x4 posts,
bracketed to the siding with four-penny nails—
balancing on opposite ends of 2x6 planking,
the scrape of the pump jacks
as the boys worked to the roof line
where they stripped, with propane torches,
decades of paint, probably leaded, bubbling blackened.

Putty knives drawn, the pine grain scorched,
paint peels fluttering to the ground like burning leaves.
clapboards smoking from the blued flame.

Eddie directing his teenage sons
to prep the siding, working with the grain,
wire brush, no goggles,
no respirators or harnesses—
Depression lessons:
hard work is good work—
his methods rare in the permissive 60s,
making men out of skinny teens, shirtless in shorts.

Practically child abuse now,
sending a boy up thirty feet to do a man's work,
but a primer in commitment, devotion to task.

Life Insurance

Eddie selling life insurance
to his Republican neighbors,
unwilling to declare his FDR
and Truman bona fides,
a Stevenson voter, for Kennedy
and Johnson, save his premium book
was fattened on the goodwill
of the West Acton Café boys
who owned the shops and garages,
filled school board seats
and the first pew at the Baptist church,
bought rounds at the VFW,
built the new developments
where Eddie stalked customers
commuting to Boston banks
or Route 128 tech firms.

1968 changed Eddie,
a veteran, a Marine,
a son of the Depression,
had little patience for hippies
or protesters even if he raised one.
He joined the Nixon crowd,
a law-and-order Republican,
a member of the Silent Majority,
unwilling to support "socialist" Humphrey
who did not serve, regardless of his excuses.

And the Boy,
before the world changed,
tallying Eddie's receipts,
the long throw of the adding machine's crank,
the tape spooling onto the floor,
as he checked each ledger entry,
the Debit Book as thick as a family Bible
recording monthly premiums
for benefits promised to Nashoba parents
dreaming for their children,
protecting bloodlines.

The Fish Store

Eddie, entrepreneur,
building a business selling exotic fish
in a makeshift basement store.
The Boy, no craftsman, jigsawed crude fishes
out of plywood scraps, hand painted,
for Eddie's signs.

The store name, long lost,
but the Man remembered
the vintage brass cash register,
the steel bulkhead entrance
to a subterranean wonderland
in a middle-class neighborhood
of Cape Cod style houses and station wagons,
backyard gardens and swing sets.

Weekends, the Boy cleaned the tanks,
sometimes stole one of Eddie's Winstons
for a sly smoke in a paradise of fishes—
Zebras, Butterflies, Gouramis,
Cichlids and Golden Barbs,
Fighting Bettas, Banded Rainbows,
otherworldly spectrums of fishes
schooling in the fluorescent waters,
weaving through diver aerators bubbling—
imagining Nemo in a conch shell helmet
twenty thousand leagues under the sea.

Dance Lessons

In the Community Center
second floor ballroom
the Boy took dance lessons,
waltzes and foxtrots, clumsily
trying to get through the night,
a few months into 6th grade,
anxious for enough training
to survive junior high school mixers.

They could be seen from Main Street,
through the Palladian windows,
boys and girls seated in folding chairs
on either side of a wide, worn oak floor,
awkwardly greeting a partner, matched.

The Boy wore his blazer,
a white shirt and skinny tie,
good shoes polished,
his nametag pinned to a lapel,
even though he knew mostly everyone,
having grown up together,
still, they seemed like strangers,
cautiously following the box step call:

Left foot forward, right foot slide step,
Then right foot back, left foot slide step,
Finding home in the closed position.

The Girl wore a beaded sweater,
black with white pearl buttons,
her white pleated skirt loose and modest,
a white blouse buttoned to the neck,

showing off a small silver cross
as if her mother dressed her for communion—
the Boy recollecting her schoolyard bully days—
her black, patent leather pumps luminous
as he and she traced a foxtrot call:

Left foot forward,
Right foot forward
Left foot sidestep left
Right foot sidestep left.

The architecture of the dancing,
the ballroom, the careful touching,
nods to those from his classes,
and those he wrestled as toddlers,
played kickball, hide-and-seek,
auditioning for a gambol
he would dance all his life,
relationships as formulaic
as the tango steps he gamely followed,
or as complicated as holding hands.

Engineer's Boots

There was an age, between the Bass Weejun
penny loafers from Concord Country Store
and the Outfitter deerskin moccasins,
for engineer's boots, black,
strapped and buckled with straight leg jeans
from the Maynard Army-Navy outlet;
between the preppy corduroys
of the Boy's coming of age, ignorant
of Freedom Marches, and patched bell-bottoms
of the 60s denouement of the Vietnam protests;
tough kid experimentation.
Engineer's boots, costumes for working class
toughs or junior highschoolers acting out
at the garage his friends rented for working
on their cars, an eternal admixture of paint,
gasoline, tires and cigarette smoke, beers
bought by one of the older kids, boasts of hemi's,
of four-barrel carburetors and chromed
rocker covers and tailpipes flared to growl.
For a year or so, the Boy talked the talk,
loved his look until the Beach Boys, Ronny
and the Daytonas, Jan & Dean
morphed into Beatle Boots, long hair, headbands,
hungry for possibilities unprescribed
by the boy-talk in small-town garages,
where the brash brag of his engineer's boots
was of no value as he imagined
a world beyond insignificance, wondering
what would he become, how would he fit in,
be a part of something not catalogued
by hairstyles, rock songs or engineer's boots.

Quarry Lands

North Acton, Harris Quarry sequestered
upside the Town Forest, chained and padlocked,
littered hillside of flawed blocks discarded,
workings camouflaged by staghorn thickets.

The Boy, on the high ledge, tell-tale drill holes
down the rock face, decades of stonecutting.
A tangle of creosoted timbers
and braided steel cables—remnants of rigs
erected for raising wedged granite slabs—
overhung the edge, the diving platform.

At the rock-edge, the Boy imagined swanning
into rippled cyan sky reflections—
other boys had made the dive and boasted
about their swim to the quarry's far side,
the abandoned truck ramp forming a crude beach,
the dive a rite of passage for the boys.

Despite his understanding, their hazing,
he hesitated, the surface forty feet down,
the rock wall curving, stretched beyond his leap,
unsure what tangle of wood, stone, and steel
lay below, cars driven over, trash buried.

He jumped, afraid to dive, momentum drove
him beyond the monsters he imagined
slept like Godzilla in Tokyo Bay.

Eyes wide open, surfacing, he swam
freestyle, right arm stroke and breath, left arm stroke
and kick, then right arm stroke, breath, kick again,
treading water, again, stroke and deep breath,
crawling onto the opposite shore, done.

He told himself he could have made the dive,
jumping was choosing, not losing his nerve!

Returning to Nashoba, an old man,
hoping to walk those same ledges again,
the place where he was tested—all vanished,
here and there a rough-hewn rock recalled
the quarry land now a sculpture garden,
modern art constructions of steel and glass
concealing both his time and the old time—
ages when boys took dares on high ledges
and raw granite was cut from the earth's heart.

Twenty-One Windows

College sophomore, the Young Man's '64,
Microbus, Sealing Wax Red—twenty-one
windows—and Chestnut Brown, sunroof manually
cranked, split windshield tilting forward,
unable to gain a shy grade at speed,
engine gone, bought from a neighbor, $1,
made it through the first winter, threw a rod,
for months, a broad-brimmed-hatted hippie's dream.

Second semester, the Beige '63
Dodge Polara Eddie sold the Young Man
for $300, his whole summer savings,
a four-door sedan, salesman's chariot,
wrecked on a late-night Burger King run.

The '65 Kombi, eleven windows,
Blue, White, and Turquoise, floorboards rotted
from winter salt with a feckless heater,
commuting to classes wrapped in quilts.

The '65 Malibu Super Sport,
Mist Blue, 283 horsepower
through his Junior and Senior college years,
stolen in '73, in Brighton.

Slogging through master's courses,
hopeless his poetry, practicing on cassettes,
living on tips and C's Gillette wages
the '68 Camaro coupe, black vinyl top,
maroon, shell bucket seats, one hundred
horsepower shy of muscle-car honors,
leaf spring snapped in an early-morning crash
on Mystic River Bridge Thruway,
after beers and backgammon.

The '69 Champagne Gold Chevelle coupe he bought
from a wannabe Guru, crowdfunding
his Krishna pilgrimage to India,
returned some months later, saffron berobed,
head shaved, begging on Boston Common.

The 70s passing in a parade
of second-hand Chevy station wagons—
Acanthus Blue and Adonis Yellow,
Ochre and Clematis Blue—hard driven,
beaters, some towed in for trade, others junked.

Two decades of Volvos—Cypress Green,
California White and Special Black,
Olive Pearl—boomer earnestness exposed,
parked side-by-side on the crushed stone driveway.

The Man, storyteller, Homer-singing
their 2005 Cadillac, new,
SRX, Raven Black, that transported
them cross country to California
where began their BMW odyssey.

Junked or sold, trade-in or new purchase,
years of transporting classmates, families,
car seats, strollers, coolers, bats, roller boards,
hockey bags, soccer balls, tennis rackets
video games, guitars, dioramas—
their biographies, paired and cross-indexed
by the used vans and coupes they owned single,
SUVs and station wagons married.

1969

The Man did not take *one small step for man,*
bathe naked in Filippini Pond at Woodstock,
program Arpanet for the DOD,
camp out on the Mall for Nixon's swearing in,
party with Ted on Chappaquiddick in 1969.

He did not fight his way up Hamburger Hill,
defend Calley for the My Lai massacre,
meet secretly with the VC in Paris;
but, with six years to go in Vietnam,
he drew a safe 209 in the draft lottery in 1969.

He did not attend Tiny Tim's wedding to Miss Vicky,
play or sing on Abbey road with the Beatles,
bed-in with John and Yoko,
co-star in *Midnight Cowboy,*
stand with the Stonewall rebels in 1969.

He was not murdered alongside Hampton,
on the jury trying Sirhan Sirhan,
on trial with the Chicago Eight,
occupying Alcatraz with *Indians of All Tribes,*
marching with the Weathermen in 1969.

He was not helter-skelter with Manson,
at the Battle of the Bogside during the Troubles,
cast on *Gunsmoke, Here's Lucy, Bonanza,*
one of *The Brady Bunch,* the Zodiac Killer,
in the Mets outfield, catching Johnson's fly ball in 1969.

He was not slaloming Loon Mountain trails
when C. caught an edge, broke her leg,
earned a hip-high cast, nursing a six-month
courtship-on-crutches, as the tale is told
by them now—about their beginnings,

A Boy's Dream of Quicksand

Recurring, the Boy's dream, the errant ball
he chased over the embankment, a swamp
primitive, a Skull Island backwater,
in real life the croquet-smooth lawn sloping
harmlessly to a stand of white birches.

In the dream, nosediving over the edge,
unable to steal a hold, into slop
sinking, deliberate his assessment,
acceptance, sunk into quicksand, the boys
on the hillside ignoring his cries, focused
on their game, no branch or rope offered,
the Boy's dream concluding, lapsing, alone.

Nashoba Ruins

Orchards left to the conquering sumac,
pastures ceded to cell base towers,
high-tension power lines and wind turbines.
The generational farms abandoned,
given back to new growth pines and waste wood,
the old growth forests long ago cut down
and turned into English ships-of-the-line.
The white pines record corn-less springs preserved
in their rings, stone walls sunken, briar-covered,
from Acton north to Townsend across the valley.
The townies claimed more land was worked
behind mule and forged harrow than Ford tractor,
even the cow corn gone, given over to brambles.
There's not Nebraska's ten feet of topsoil,
but almost three feet of blood, manure, cornstalks
and the bequests of Pequod and Plymouth corpses.
The Young Man could not smell the fish heads
improving the poor ground at Plymouth,
and had no dream of Merrimack thanksgivings.
Nashoba farmers failing in his youth, gone now,
never intending to feed more than the family
with extra for the Chelsea Markets and seed.
Homesteads auctioned after the farmers moved on,
Sold the posts and beams raising the barn and house,
along with the machinery, the tools, the stuff of a working life.
Salvage used in "rustic" man caves, in new houses.
the rubble-stone foundations carried off
to gravel pits and cracked into crushed stone.

Rob

Rob

We met In the parking lot, Freshman Week,
unpacking gear, clothes, typewriters, and books
crammed into our parents' station wagons,
natural best friends from our first handshake,
two of us, long-haired hippie wannabes
in a murder of crew cuts, comb backs, buzz cuts—
Dean demanding we conform to the code,
haircut before our first class, preserving
decorum, our virtuous campus life—
we reveled in it all, patched jeans and fringe.

Juniors, we moved off-campus, commuters,
painted a suite of rooms, high-hippie style,
yellow Hammer & Sickle on a red field
opposing the Stars & Stripes, newspaper
headlines papering a wall in a mad
collage with aluminum foil stapled
to the ceiling, mood lights in corners.

There was the night we played "Let It Be,"
"I'm So Tired," "Strawberry Fields Forever"
backwards because Paul was dead;
the mescaline and LSD trips at the maze
at Vanderbilt's Breakers or Dartmouth Woods
listening to Ten Years After and Ten Wheel Drive;
or Country Joe at Psychedelic Supermarket
the Who performing *Tommy* at Lansdowne;
Janis at the Music Hall in the Back Bay;
Times Square on New Year's Eve
where we fought over which bar to go to;
a four-year odyssey testing limits.

Graduating into the world, no lanes
for English or Sociology grads,
after months at home both working odd jobs—
construction, factory assembly lines—
we drifted into Boston, without plans,
me writing, Rob painting, without success,
trying to make our way, stymied, stalled out.

Celia and I moved to Marblehead,
other friends matched up, moved on, Rob went home,
to his mother's house, to paint and read,
to re-educate and renew himself,
and we began a decade of letter
writing, poet and painter pursuing
understandings, a "duologue" on art.

Letters from Rob

Reluctant to write without painterly
stuff, something artful to share, to please you,
but continuous contact not content
urges conversation given concerns—
your car, your lack of work, circumstances.
How does your poetry fare these days, frère?
This capon finds himself apart, painting,
sketching four or five hours a day, walking,
active, developing, thoughts aplenty,
absent organized, artistic outcomes.
What have you been reading, while I fossick
on Pound, some Yeats . . . please voyage to Dartmouth—
Your Robert, January 10, 1975

Searching for books on Delacroix, bingeing,
struggling with bills, student loans, bullish
on my art despite the cash deficits,
lately rediscovered walking in woods
of my kid-hood, conjuring trysts with girls
walking the Paskamanset River trails—
Your Robert, January 31, 1975

You and I have a selfishness
of sacred ground in common, not meeting
enough but enthusiastically.
Recently, some difficulty working—
Your Buffon, February 11, 1975

Arnold Bennett and Elbert Hubbard journals, Martindale's
Man, the Renaissance, *consume my soul.*
A swamp, awe-full of the Masters' paintings,
seduced by this universe of greatness,
I find myself unable to concentrate on my work
but have started a 5 x 3 homage to Rubens.

Your admiration of Watteau on the Providence trip,
truth, you lack a feel for fine oil sketches,
missing the intent, the sometimes careful,
often free-form fancies, trial, and error
dance of the strokes, the color confusion.
Walking along the old hurricane dike
we chanced upon a snowy owl carcass—
Your Rob, or whatever my name is, March 3, 1975

Received the book, retiring safe, wide-eyed,
sheltered in bed beneath the reading lamp.
Visit, yes. Your decision, working man
deserves his rest and solitude foremost.
Wandering the museum—Fuseli, Stubbs,
Rubens and Géricault—uncovering
E. Delacroix's romantic horses—
Roberto, March 4, 1975

Stampless, stymied, unwilling to write more,
concealing a hoard of partial letters,
unsound thoughts best revealed over coffee,
but your letter arrived, here's what I have—
Your great return to school does you good stead
and an intensity of good purpose.
My favorite word this week is buzzard
and I've been painting aged fishermen,
imaging tales told, traditions they held,
drawing their hands, correct in the telling,
the chorus of the seas, rhythm of sails.
D.H. Lawrence's poems leave me gasping
"I remember the scream of a rabbit
As I went through a wood at midnight . . ."
I must finish, my message will be delivered
If it is my mailman mother driving—
Rob, March 25, 1975

I have so much to write but moving day
is upon me, patience, until Tuesday,
I wanted to make progress with Hamsun
and send you and Celia a drawing
in thanks for a lovely weekend,
It was large of both of you to embrace me.
Hopefulness, a glimmer, for the Red Sox.
Alan gossips that you haven't written.
Reading constant, St. Mar, The Man who Died,
Aldus Huxley's The Devils of Loudon—
A handshake in thought, Your Robert, April 14, 1975

And now Knut Hamsun, Hunger *and* Growth of the Soil,
pencil and sketchbook roaming New Bedford,
looking for contrasts worthy of a page,
our Red Sox nine, heroics to horrors—
Rob, May 1, 1975

You said they were good little trees, I worked
to reflect, the sky yellower, blended;
Put some heart, some paint into Mom's portrait
after sampling "The Discourses" of Joshua Reynolds
and the student notes in the margin.
I practiced scumbling my brush recklessly
drenched, dragged across my primed canvas,
revealing the underlayment in the scrawl.
Discovered a shed, at the edge of a posted field,
slipped in and sketched it anyway.
Won a prize at a cookout flying a glider the furthest!
Goodness did I soak up the adoration—
Rob, June 1, 1975

A Man strives to become graceful and strong.
I cannot believe that your writing will stop,
a severe case of university brain;
You, always the well-read pessimist,
me trending toward a dumb optimism.
Your signature seems calligraphic, pure,
I've been practicing although left-handed.
Entitling these pages "Homage to Jonathan"
come and get me if you dare—
Robert, June 17, 1975

*The Bicentennial looms, I have a booth
and now must ready 50 pieces by August.
But my stay at Joslin interferes, a month of tuning,
where I hope to finish the consignment.
You and Celia are well I hope?
You are still in the taxicab snarl?
Men should communicate lying flat,
backs on the earth, angled acutely
to indicate our unique selves,
counting the clouds and grunting like animals—
Rob,* Spring 1976

*At long last home, a splendid state of disarray.
Invested $150 and brought 2 charcoal drawings, framed,
3 oils on canvas and 7 drawings to a show—a humiliation
as I saw table after table of professionally presented work.
I've met a woman with mysterious eyes—
My deepest feelings to you and Celia,* April 26, 1976

*Another week, drifting on a barge of ill-luck,
I sit, stomach a-churn, soulful;
Frustrated not that we are mediocre, not famous
but the doubt we share in transition
to competent craftsmen.
Have we ever finished anything?
Like Gainsborough, will we sacrifice 10 years
for a single outcome, then abandon it?
I repainted that sky you studied
and the middle field, coming to realize how hard
the work is and must be.*

*I hope you will be accepting myself next weekend,
if you are able to avoid Sunday cabbing.
I'll wring out your poetic wrinkles in person—
Rob,* May 24, 1976

*Co-owner of a portrait studio!
Everything, every little thing
makes a space safe to work, to paint through winter
with a partner and critic, companion.
I have ideas, good ideas, stories.
If you were here, we would talk solemnly,
laugh together, out loud, wrestle the facts.
Perhaps, in some distant future living
Within walking distance, if you are willing,
Meeting in fierce duels, young gods, wielding language.
Weary, can go no longer. Blah, blah, blah.
See you soon—
Rob,* September 21, 1976

*Home from lunch and finding yourself in the mailbox,
glad you two are getting married
although I would prefer a well-paced string of other women,
call me, after the Holidays, save me
from roaming Marblehead streets untethered,
blind as Homer—
Rob,* December 1976

Jonathan, quit my job in the plastic
factory, now quite poor, freedom at last
to read your poems I put aside during
my last month of incoherence, leaving
for the library, a bus ride, to research
Oceanus *and thus begin—*
Rob, Spring 1977

Jonathan, reading you:
"Preaching from heather-steeped, humped and rearing brae"
a fine line and closing with "in Black Latin" *silent and final.*
"Soon a match roars, firing wind, searing him a halo,"
from the third stanza, a clear, image.
Not getting the use of "fay" *an odd word to my ear*
and I'm lost in your theory of the connectivity
of land, God and men thus a painter not a poet.
Three more oils, one a week.
and my hatred of Arthur Gordon Pym,
Fate handing us books from the hands of friends.
Finished the landscape you admired,
not so much the black water—
$75 plus three more commissions.
Hoping you valued my critical reading; I felt your passion.
I find words so entangling—
Rob, Summer 1977

*Come down before the weather runs away,
the forests are still yellow and brown.
Read* Gone With The Wind, *what of your poems?
The one you started in England, I liked,
but can't recall the one you last called out—
a man's work is metamorphosis,
rather than individual performance,
Am I forgiven—
Rob,* Fall 1977

*Its high time you wrote me a slender line.
Are you still an executive, or higher?
Remember, you can't keep nature out.
Are you still driven, to what extent?
Write me—
Rob,* September 13, 1979

He Took Off the Old Coat

The Carriage House

Nashoba, the farmhouse, white clapboard,
narrow as a Louisiana shotgun shack,
married to a hip-roofed, lofted barn,
and The Carriage House, store, detached,
where Dot pursued her independence,
the antique pickers coming and going,
the collectibles trade satisfying
her need to own something outside her home.
A century after the last surrey was winched up the ramp,
the buggy Eddie bought for marketing
posed for the tourists on Great Road, leather
benches, dashboard, tail board and shafts
the same weathered grey, staged by the hand pump,
handle long detached from piston, rust red.
Sometimes, the Young Man looked after Dot's store,
recalled the scolding he took for selling
her Shirley Temple pitcher for $10
when she, fan girl, wanted $20,
her grumbling brief, she forgot to price it.

Stone Wall, Poetry

Eddie, 2nd Marines, stingy with praise.
Dottie telling the Young Man, long after,
how Eddie retold the story of restoring
the fallen stone wall behind the Carriage House,
levering toppled boulders, splitting rocks
into smaller wedges with cold steel chisel
and crack hammer, driving the pieces home
with a seven-pound sledge or the butt end
of the pry bar he had used to raise them
from the years of moss, roots and compacted
leaves where they lay after the ice storm
waters expanded into the crevices,
unmade what the Farmer had wrought.

Despite the bruises, the aching back and knees,
the casual scrape from a careless swing,
the Young Man liked repairing the walls.
Yet building walls, no matter how upright,
sacrificed time to put his shoulder
to his poetry, the heavy lifting,
dry-fitting edits, testing, chiseling lines,
stanzas, every bit as backbreaking
as bringing cold steel to obdurate rock,
perfecting words into verses fitting
like fussy stones smartly set in a wall.

Haggling

Eddie and Dot—American pickers
before television made heroes
of junkyard scavengers and hoarders—
handshake deals, elaborate narratives
of two-faced sellers and trusting buyers.
At Brimfield or Hollis or a Concord
estate sale avoiding the guys working
the margins in the bidding pool, the back
of the auction tent where free markets ruled
and episodic men bargained for leverage.
The Man dabbled in the trade, paid some dues
in trips to the North Country, the Berkshires,
the Cape and Northeast Kingdom, his eye trained
to suss American Art Pottery—
matte green glazes, the shoulder of a well-turned vase,
the tell-tale flash of a flower pattern, molded—
from the detritus of garage sales and flea markets;
Hours searching boxes of vinyl records
for a missing Lee Morgan or Coltrane
to fill gaps in his hard bop collection.
He haggled when the seller deserved it,
when a fair, honest price was not offered.
He relished winning, but not at all costs,
money probably left on the table,
still an understanding created when, checking
new arrivals, that seller had something for him
and that he would pay well for what he liked.

The Fence on Sedgewick Drive

The fence we built was white cedar, eight foot
boards, shiplap, double gated, our acre
well-defined and well-lit by carriage lamps.
But then our neighbors, not sharing our pride
in good fences, shunned us, Frost all the same.
No moralizing, no antipathy
for our good neighbors behind our good fence,
where, seemingly unengaged, secretive
beneath a latticework of oak branches,
the Man crazed with yardwork, our neighbors
not lending their soft hands to the mending
and mowing, the leaf raking, the sawing
and splitting of limbs felled by New England winters.
The good fence now serving to define
our differences, made us adversaries,
improved our acre but Impoverished
our neighborhood, rift widening yearly,
until moving west to Silicon Valley
where neighbors' fences, walls and hedges
line the tight lanes of neighboring bastions.

Abandonment

Do parents, self-obsessed,
Merit our achievements,
Left on our own, survivors?

What do we owe our parents?
Blood humors, elemental,
But love's blank check?

If in hindsight, it all worked out,
If we succeed, their hand surely helping,
How much is due to nurturing?

Abandoned, at least in part,
Was it our nature to persevere?
Or was the ambition in their blood?

Waiting for Owls

We fixed the Owl House high enough
in the magnolia, blooming
beneath the Canary Island Pine,
above the grevilia's purple spray
outside our kitchen window, in full view
but far from the deep pine woods or barn loft
where any owl might find comfort.

Celia and I anticipated
the screech owl's whistling,
insistent, a trilling progression of chords,
like a post-bop pianist banging away,
call and answer with the double bass and drummer,
birdsong, nature is as Nature does.
We are here, hear us! We hunt!

We waited the years, impatient
for the pandemic passing, the Owl House
witnessing the magnolia's bloom
secure in the woody, broad leaf canopy.
We sometimes hear owls up in the redwoods
bordering the eighth tee, on quiet nights,
our proffer unrequited, nest unwitnessed.
Inflight, purposeful, yellow-eyed
On the wing, silent, communion,
We hunt, we are hunters, Amen.

Nashoba Waters

The Man jonesed lures, rods and reels, fishing gear
at flea markets decades after he last
walked the coarse shorelines of Nashoba ponds,
threaded the willow tangles, cradling gear,
along brooks spilling, wrangling through boulders.
Daredevles, Syclopses, Slammers, Sonics,
Bangtails, Rooster Tails and Switcheroos,
Jawbreakers, Creek Creatures, Bang-O-Lures
Hot Lips, Invincibles, Flash Dancers, Woodwalkers
sorted in tackle boxes side-by-side
on garage shelving along with poles in cases
and a dozen or more fly reels, spinning reels
and a box dedicated to trout flies, streamers,
Feathergirls, Quill Gordons, Blue-Wings, Caddises,
Carey Specials, Coachmans, Alexandras and Woolly Worms.

He examined the hoard on occasion,
chose a box, slid out a lure tray and inspected
the paint and barbs, looking over the swivels
and the leaders, the unopened coils of line,
wondering if there would come a rift in time
when he might again wade a trout stream
high up in the White Mountain watershed,
looking for that perfect eddy to make his first cast.

No Tear Goes Wasted

Late, after dinner, the landscape lighting
washing the palm fronds, a southwest breeze cool,
inspiring the wind chimes banging, clanging,
listening to Iris DeMent, *My Life,*
The Shores of Jordan, the Poet humbled
by her Appalachian grace.
He could not point to, recall, invent
a moment where he volunteered his tears
in defense of another, no angels'
wings would carry his soul to Jordan,
not his reward nor ambition as he, graceless,
heard her singing and imagined
her dancing on the riverbank.

Crows Crowded into the Redwood Tree Tops

Crows crowded into the redwood tree tops
out of sky-blue, cloud-swept heavens, singles,
in pairs, by threes if Hitchcock directing,
until two dozen more crammed the branches;
Then all but one surrendered its watch,
only to return by twos and by threes.
And the Man saw the object of their ire,
a reddish shadow in the blood-red leaves
of a Thundercloud Plum beneath their post
that resolved into a red-shouldered hawk,
wordlessly gliding over the roof-ridge,
skimming the pool and then soaring,
a mousey prize in one yellowed talon,
into a Sitka Spruce fixing the lot,
pausing to adjust its hold, then away,
until it disappeared into the marine layer
flooding the foothills, across the valley,
the protesting crows screeching, bested.

He Took Off the Old Coat

In the pandemic years, the Man retired,
no longer empowered to lead hundreds,
a dozen suits dry cleaned, sheathed in vinyl
scabbards, hung side-by-side since 2020,
closeted with his Santoni slip-ons;
His button-down shirts, pastel, striped and white,
primly starched and stacked in the top drawer,
in their plastic sleeves, arrayed blue-to-white.
As he stared at his hands on the keyboard,
older they seemed, veined and oddly thinner,
he realized he hadn't worn a watch
in three years—the large, black-dialed Movado,
the chic gold-bezeled Longines, the Rado
and the Seiko that Celia gifted him
for some past milestones, maybe a birthday—
all that analog instrumentation
locked away, marking the hour and minute
each watch battery wore down and time stopped.
But he had moved on, put on a new coat,
made to measure at first as if scissored
from a Sears catalog pattern thumb-tacked
to an ironing board; sewing verses,
unpicking feedback, listening, mending—
cross-stitching, tailoring lapels, vents, cuffs,
hemming in pentameter, iambic.

About the Author

Jonathan Clark Patrick is the author of *Songs Presidential* (Kelsay Books, 2022). His fascination with the American presidency began during his childhood in the region around Boston, where so many key events in U.S. political history have occurred. He now resides in the San Francisco Bay area with his wife of forty-seven years. Patrick drove a cab during graduate school, writing his first poems while studying American literature. He put aside his writing as he became more successful in his professional services career. Inspired by the momentous 2008 election, Patrick returned in *Songs Presidential* to his lifelong goal of exploring the interaction between history and poetry. *Out of Nashoba* is a continuation of his personal journey started in *Songs Presidential*.

www.ingramcontent.com/pod-product-compliance
Lightning Source LLC
Chambersburg PA
CBHW031204160426
43193CB00008B/495